MW00529117

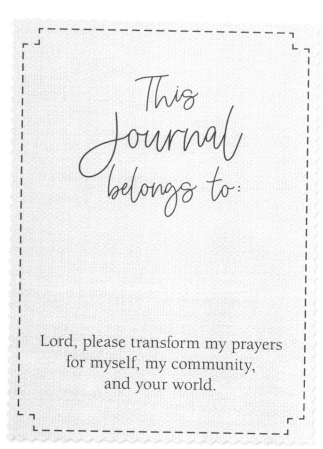

This
Journal
belongs to:

Lord, please transform my prayers
for myself, my community,
and your world.

Our Daily Bread
Publishing™

Beloved

Then Christ will make his home in your hearts as you trust in him. Your roots will grow down into God's love and keep you strong. And may you have the power to understand, as all God's people should, how wide, how long, how high, and how deep his love is. May you experience the love of Christ, though it is too great to understand fully. Then you will be made complete with all the fullness of life and power that comes from God.

EPHESIANS 3:17–19 NLT

> "Be still, and know that I am God."
>
> PSALM 46:10 KJV

....

....

....

....

....

....

....

....

....

....

....

....

Reflections

God loves me; my Savior, Jesus, intercedes and
advocates for me; and the Holy Spirit groans
for me, comforts, leads, and teaches me.

Reflections

"Who then will condemn us? No one—for Christ Jesus died for us and was raised to life for us, and he is sitting in the place of honor at God's right hand, pleading for us."

ROMANS 8:34 NLT

Reflections

My entrance into heaven and being able to stand before the Father is because of Jesus's work on the cross, not my merit or self-effort.

Reflections

"For it is by grace you have been saved,
through faith—and this is not from
yourselves, it is the gift of God—not by
works, so that no one can boast."

EPHESIANS 2:8–9 NIV

God loves me, prays for me, and longs to commune with me because of the richness of His mercy. Jesus is my Mediator, communicating what is on the Father's heart to me and my heart to Him.

....

....

....

....

....

....

....

....

....

Reflections

"We do not know what we ought to pray for, but the Spirit himself intercedes for us through wordless groans."

ROMANS 8:26 NIV

Reflections

God reminds me to lay down my anxieties; to stop scrambling, and to sit amazed at His activity.

Reflections

"Because of the LORD's great love we are not consumed, for his compassions never fail. They are new every morning; great is your faithfulness."

LAMENTATIONS 3:22–23 NIV

Thank you, Lord, for upholding us as you call the lost and lonely into your arms.

....

....

....

....

....

....

....

....

....

....

....

....

Reflections

"For the LORD your God is living among you. He is a mighty savior. He will take delight in you with gladness. With his love, he will calm all your fears. He will rejoice over you with joyful songs."

ZEPHANIAH 3:17 NLT

Reflections

God is seeking, calling, and waiting for me.
God holds me in the palm of His loving hand.

Reflections

"This is what the LORD says: . . . 'See, I have engraved you on the palms of my hands.'"

ISAIAH 49:8, 16 NIV

Reflections

No other love compares to God's love.

Reflections

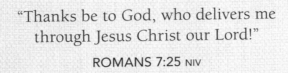

"Thanks be to God, who delivers me
through Jesus Christ our Lord!"

ROMANS 7:25 NIV

....

....

....

....

....

....

....

....

....

....

....

Reflections

God sincerely desires a relationship with me,
cultivated through prayer.

Reflections

"So now there is no condemnation for those who belong to Christ Jesus."

ROMANS 8:1 NLT

Reflections

God is not working hard at loving me;
it is His pleasure.

Reflections

Reflections

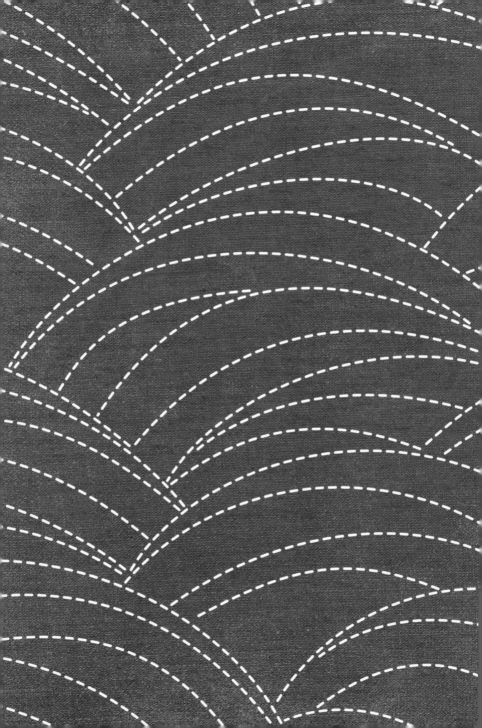

Beautiful

I will praise thee; for I am fearfully
and wonderfully made: marvellous
are thy works; and that my soul
knoweth right well. My substance
was not hid from thee, when I
was made in secret, and curiously
wrought in the lowest parts of
the earth. Thine eyes did see my
substance, yet being unperfect; and
in thy book all my members were
written, which in continuance were
fashioned, when as yet there was
none of them. How precious also are
thy thoughts unto me, O God! how
great is the sum of them!

PSALM 139:14–17 KJV

Jesus is alive and is interceding on my behalf.

....

....

....

....

....

....

....

....

....

....

....

Reflections

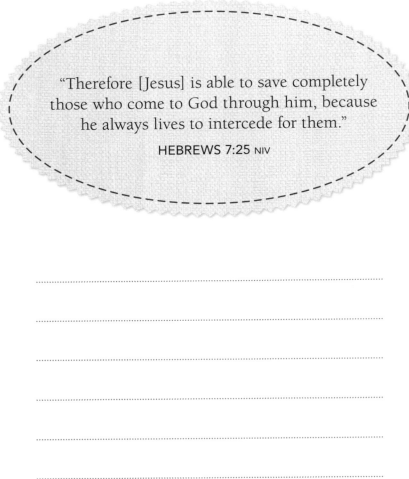

"Therefore [Jesus] is able to save completely those who come to God through him, because he always lives to intercede for them."

HEBREWS 7:25 NIV

Reflections

The heavenly Father is *my* Father, and has promised to provide for me. He will direct my path and will guide me even when I don't understand everything.

....

....

....

....

....

....

....

....

....

....

Reflections

"Trust in the LORD with all thine heart;
and lean not unto thine own understanding.
In all thy ways acknowledge him,
and he shall direct thy paths."

PROVERBS 3:5–6 KJV

Reflections

God has always, in His omniscience and love,
had good plans for me.

....

....

....

....

....

....

....

....

....

....

Reflections

> "'For I know the plans I have for you,' declares the LORD, 'plans to prosper you and not to harm you, plans to give you hope and a future.'"
>
> **JEREMIAH 29:11** NIV

Reflections

I willingly pray for others, as I am *your child.*
My simple prayer rests in you.

Reflections

"But when you pray, go into your room, close the door and pray to your Father, who is unseen. Then your Father, who sees what is done in secret, will reward you."

MATTHEW 6:6 NIV

Reflections

God intercedes, restores, renews,
and reconfigures me.

Reflections

Reflections

God cares for me on paths that lead
through valleys of loss and provides
His joy and restoration.

Reflections

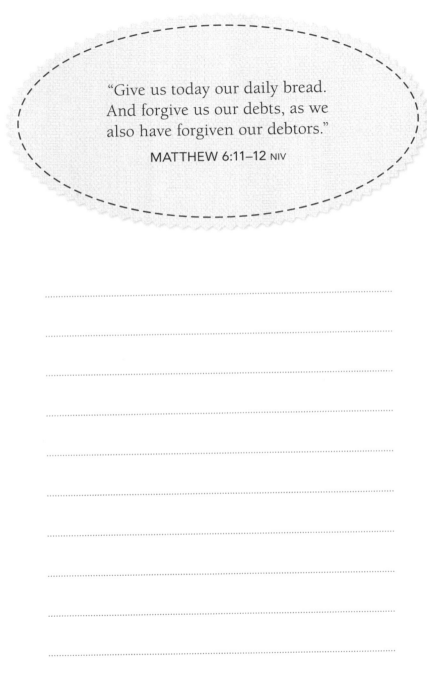

"Give us today our daily bread. And forgive us our debts, as we also have forgiven our debtors."

MATTHEW 6:11–12 NIV

Reflections

My attitudes can testify to God's empowerment
and grace. God is interceding for me;
refashioning, repairing, and altering me.

....

....

....

....

....

....

....

....

....

....

....

Reflections

"And lead us not into temptation,
but deliver us from the evil one.' For if you
forgive other people when they sin against you,
your heavenly Father will also forgive you."

MATTHEW 6:13–14 NIV

Reflections

I can rest in Christ's prayers for me,
and in His power at work in and through me.

Reflections

> "For your Creator will be your husband;
> the LORD of Heaven's Armies is his name!
> He is your Redeemer, the Holy One of Israel,
> the God of all the earth."
>
> ISAIAH 54:5 NLT

....

....

....

....

....

....

....

....

....

....

Reflections

> *Jehovah Rapha*, "God our healer," is able to
> turn around tragic life events.

Reflections

"[The Lord] heals the brokenhearted and binds up their wounds."

PSALM 147:3 NIV

Reflections

Praise you, oh Lord, that you have your eyes
on the forgotten, the broken, and the hated;
that we are loved deeply by you.

Reflections

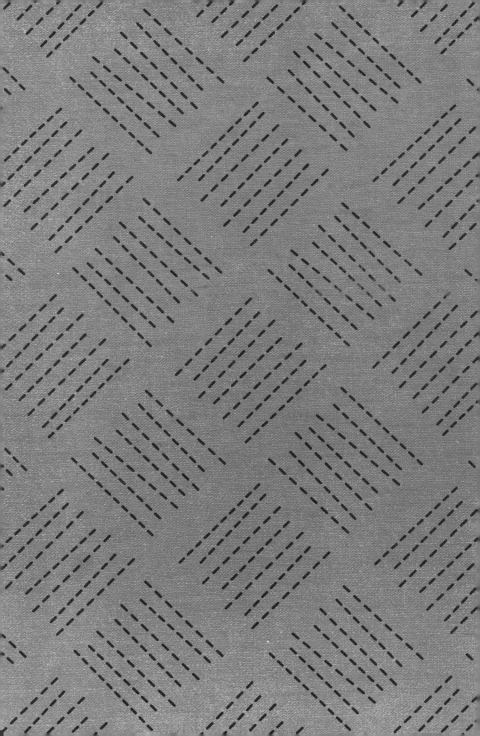

Brave

I say to myself, "The Lord is my inheritance; therefore, I will hope in him!" The Lord is good to those who depend on him, to those who search for him. So it is good to wait quietly for salvation from the Lord.

LAMENTATIONS 3:24–26 NLT

....

....

....

....

....

....

....

....

....

....

....

Reflections

God is still God, and able to help the
betrayed and rejected.

Reflections

> "I have loved you with an everlasting love."
>
> JEREMIAH 31:3 NIV

Reflections

The woman from Samaria did not go looking
for Jesus; rather, He found her (see John 4).

Reflections

"Come, see a man who told me
everything I ever did.
Could this be the Messiah?"

JOHN 4:29 NIV

Reflections

God's open arms are never closed.

Reflections

You have searched me, LORD,
and you know me.
You know when I sit and when I rise;
you perceive my thoughts from afar.

PSALM 139:1–2 NIV

Reflections

The Lord never rebukes us when we seek Him sincerely. He waits for us to turn to Him even when we don't know what or how to pray.

....

....

....

....

....

....

....

....

....

Reflections

> "But ye shall receive power, after that the
> Holy Ghost is come upon you."
>
> ACTS 1:8 KJV

Reflections

The Holy Spirit is in our prayers and assists in all our ways—even when we are unaware of His presence.

Reflections

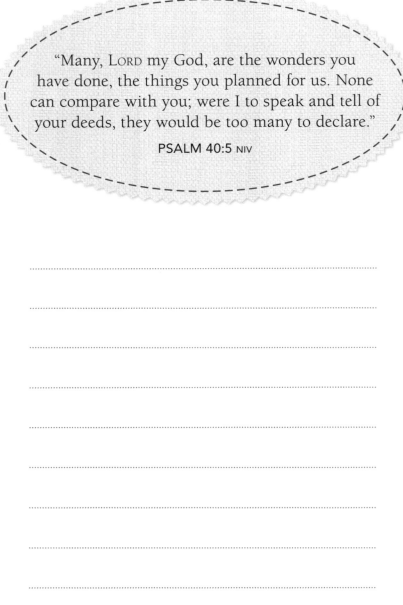

"Many, LORD my God, are the wonders you have done, the things you planned for us. None can compare with you; were I to speak and tell of your deeds, they would be too many to declare."

PSALM 40:5 NIV

Reflections

God invites us to bring everything to Him.
He already has great plans for our lives.

Reflections

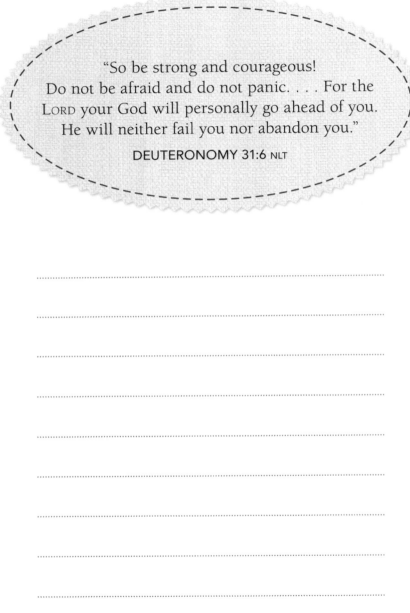

"So be strong and courageous!
Do not be afraid and do not panic. . . . For the
LORD your God will personally go ahead of you.
He will neither fail you nor abandon you."

DEUTERONOMY 31:6 NLT

Reflections

We can expect God not only to answer the request we've made but also to answer requests we haven't thought to ask.

....

....

....

....

....

....

....

....

....

....

Reflections

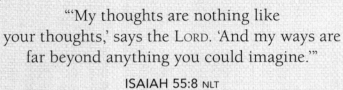

"'My thoughts are nothing like
your thoughts,' says the Lord. 'And my ways are
far beyond anything you could imagine.'"

ISAIAH 55:8 NLT

....

....

....

....

....

....

....

....

....

....

Reflections

God welcomes me to talk to Him and
invites me to listen.

....

....

....

....

....

....

....

....

....

....

Reflections

> "This is the confidence we have in approaching God: that if we ask anything according to his will, he hears us."
>
> **1 JOHN 5:14** NIV

Reflections

The God-ness of God is never diluted
in my waiting and neither is His call
on my life watered down when He
doesn't answer quickly.

....

....

....

....

....

....

....

....

....

....

Reflections

> "And if we know that [God] hears us—whatever we ask—we know that we have what we asked of him."
>
> 1 JOHN 5:15 NIV

Reflections

Blessed

Keep on asking, and you will receive what you ask for. Keep on seeking, and you will find. Keep on knocking, and the door will be opened to you. For everyone who asks, receives. Everyone who seeks, finds. And to everyone who knocks, the door will be opened.

You parents—if your children ask for a loaf of bread, do you give them a stone instead? Or if they ask for a fish, do you give them a snake? Of course not! So if you sinful people know how to give good gifts to your children, how much more will your heavenly Father give good gifts to those who ask him.

MATTHEW 7:7–11 NLT

No matter what kind of grief, our God is always present; He turns "mourning into dancing" (Psalm 30:11 KJV).

....

....

....

....

....

....

....

....

....

....

Reflections

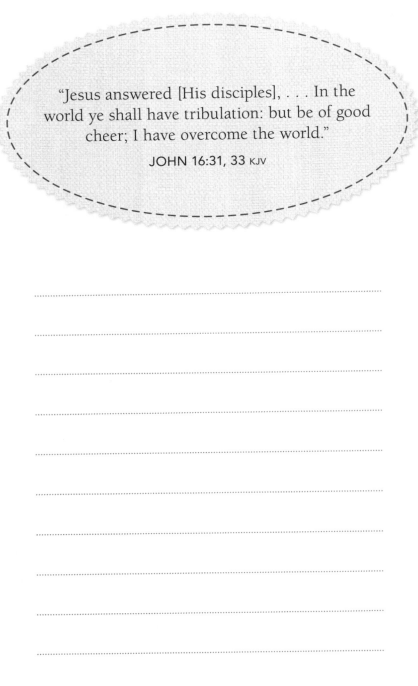

"Jesus answered [His disciples], . . . In the world ye shall have tribulation: but be of good cheer; I have overcome the world."

JOHN 16:31, 33 KJV

Reflections

Honestly communicating our heart before the Lord is the medicine and treatment for deep heartaches.

Reflections

> "God's peace . . . will guard your hearts and minds as you live in Christ Jesus."
>
> PHILIPPIANS 4:7 NLT

Reflections

Abba Father, thank you for your peace
freely given to us.

Reflections

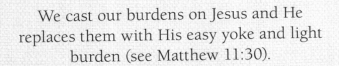

We cast our burdens on Jesus and He replaces them with His easy yoke and light burden (see Matthew 11:30).

....

....

....

....

....

....

....

....

....

....

Reflections

"Keep thy heart with all diligence;
for out of it are the issues of life."

PROVERBS 4:23 KJV

Reflections

The power of God resides in us as Christian believers; we are not helpless against negative thoughts.

....

....

....

....

....

....

....

....

....

....

....

"Now faith is the substance of things hoped for,
the evidence of things not seen."

HEBREWS 11:1 KJV

Reflections

God wants us to ask questions
and to say what's on our heart and
mind. He desires to answer us.

Reflections

Reflections

> "Give all your worries and cares to God,
> for he cares about you."
>
> **1 PETER 5:7** NLT

Reflections

"For the eyes of the Lord are over the righteous, and his ears are open unto their prayers: but the face of the Lord is against them that do evil."

1 PETER 3:12 KJV

Reflections

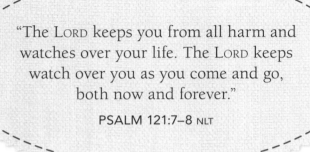

"The LORD keeps you from all harm and watches over your life. The LORD keeps watch over you as you come and go, both now and forever."

PSALM 121:7–8 NLT

"Now all glory to God, who is able, through his mighty power at work within us, to accomplish infinitely more than we might ask or think."

EPHESIANS 3:20 NLT

Reflections

> "Devote yourselves to prayer,
> being watchful and thankful."
>
> COLOSSIANS 4:2 NIV

Reflections

"Pray in the Spirit at all times and on every occasion. Stay alert and be persistent in your prayers for all believers everywhere."

EPHESIANS 6:18 NLT

Reflections

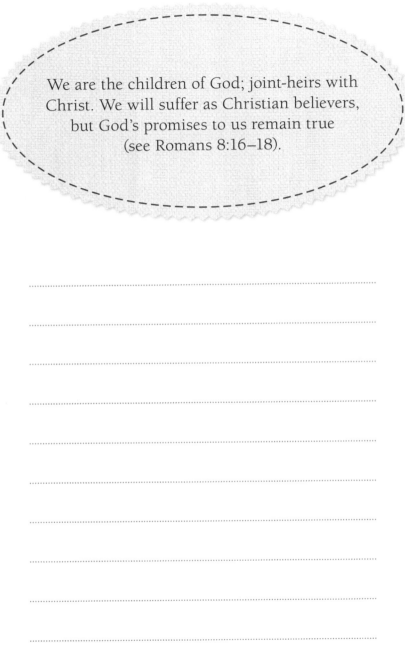

We are the children of God; joint-heirs with Christ. We will suffer as Christian believers, but God's promises to us remain true (see Romans 8:16–18).

....

....

....

....

....

....

....

....

....

Reflections

Bold

For though we live in the world, we do not wage war as the world does. The weapons we fight with are not the weapons of the world. On the contrary, they have divine power to demolish strongholds. We demolish arguments and every pretension that sets itself up against the knowledge of God, and we take captive every thought to make it obedient to Christ.

2 CORINTHIANS 10:3–5 NIV